NEW ORDER OF WORSHIP

Thomas Enow

New Order of Worship

Trilogy Christian Publishers A Wholly Owned Subsidary of Trinity Broadcasting Network

2442 Michelle Drive Tustin, CA 92780

Copyright © 2021 by Thomas Enow

Rights Department, 2442 Michelle Drive, Tustin, CA 92780.

Trilogy Christian Publishing/TBN and colophon are trademarks of Trinity Broadcasting Network.

Cover design by: Grant Swank

For information about special discounts for bulk purchases, please contact Trilogy Christian Publishing.

Trilogy Disclaimer: The views and content expressed in this book are those of the author and may not necessarily reflect the views and doctrine of Trilogy Christian Publishing or the Trinity Broadcasting Network.

Manufactured in the United States of America

10 9 8 7 6 5 4 3 2 1

Library of Congress Cataloging-in-Publication Data is available.

ISBN: 978-1-63769-334-6

E-ISBN: 978-1-63769-335-3

Contents

Dedication

I dedicate this book to the Holy Spirit for His wisdom and inspiration and also to the MIGAD Blood TV Team for their fervent prayers for me and precious seeds to favor the poor and needy into God-ordained ministry.

Thank you for holding on to this mission!

Introduction

Over the years, believers are taught to engage the force of fasting and prayer to break down strongholds and secure divine intervention. Yes, I believe in the power of prayer, and even Jesus taught us to pray and equally instructed us to pray ceaselessly. However, the Scripture is replete with other spiritual weapons of war that most believers hardly engage. One of such is worship.

Everybody worships; it's a question of what or who. Worship is one of the most used words in the Body of Christ today. To some, it is just a church word mentioned when it's time to sing. To others, it's an action to commence a Christian gathering. This misguided ideology of worship has relegated its potency to the background in our overall Christian experience.

I love Psalm 22:3; it says, "But you are holy, you who inhabit the praises of Israel." Did you see that?

Worship is a quick way to usher in the Majesty of God into your situation and circumstance. And when the Monarch of the Universe steps in, expect every contrary situation to step out unannounced— awesome! Worship is the deepest dimension of intimacy between God and man. What more, when Jesus came, He revealed to us in John chapter 4 that the Father is seeking men and women, male and female, boys and girls from every nation, tribe, and race who will worship Him as a lifestyle. Amazing!

However, understanding is vital to enjoying the blessings of the kingdom. The Psalmist said, "...give me understanding, and I shall live" (Psalm 119:144). This goes to show that our level of understanding of kingdom principles determines our fruitfulness.

And there is no greater void in the Body of Christ today than a declined hunger for understanding.

That is why I've carefully written this book. I seek to fill up the void that has kept many saints from living a life of acceptable worship to the Father.

You see, we are created as worship-beings. The Bible clearly says in Isaiah 43:21, "This people have I formed for myself; they shall shew forth my praise." The true essence of the breath of the Almighty in our body is to praise Him. A.W. Tozer once said, "Without worship, we go about miserable." And that is the challenge today. A lot of people think they can get satisfaction from things, titles, and possessions. But even after all that, there still remains an unfillable emptiness in them that only true worship can fill. Charles Spurgeon also said, "Nothing teaches us about the preciousness of the Creator as much as when we learn the emptiness of everything else."

The encounter between Jesus and the Samaritan woman in John chapter 4 illustrates this better. She told Jesus of their usual and regular journey to Jerusalem to worship the Father, yet when she met Jesus, she still had a desperation to be filled with the fullness of God. She eventually appeals in John 4:15, "Sir, give me this water, that I thirst not, neither come hither to draw." Friend, only a U-turn to the right order of worship can make up for the lack of joy and fulfillment that permeates men's hearts today.

Therefore, get set for a new light. Get set to know the truth that sets free. Get set for a launch into a life of joy full of unspeakable glory. Get set for a spiritual inoculation and transplant of divine truth that can set you free.

I know you may be in an unpleasant situation that has defiled all medication. Perhaps you are indebted to the tune of millions of dollars, and you don't seem to know the way out. Or maybe some circumstances of life have weighed you down. I congratulate you because you are holding the book that proffers a solution that may have defied all odds.

Worship looks too simple but carries divine potency that can clear off barriers on your path if engaged in truth and by faith. Perhaps no story in the Bible better illustrates the power of ordered worship than Paul and Silas in the book of Acts chapter 16. These men were arrested and due for execution for preaching the Gospel. But the night before their execution, these men knew better. Despite their situation, the Bible says they prayed, but when it seems their desired result wasn't forthcoming, they switched the gear completely to praises rather than giving up and complaining. Eventually, in Act 16:26, the ible says, "And suddenly there was a great earthquake so that the foundations of the prison were shaken: and immediately all the doors were opened, and everyone's bands were loosed." *Hallelujah*!

It's easy to sing when the chains are off; it's easy to dance when the doors have opened in our favor, but what's your response when the chips are down? These two giants of faith demonstrated that when you desire to clear off limitations, you should engage in true worship of God.

What more, worship is not limited to singing and dancing. Oh yes! What are the other dimensions of worship? Let's dive in as the Holy Spirit begins to expound in our hearts the efficacy of ordered worship and the accompanying blessings.

Chapter One

My Transformation Experience

I'd like to start this life-changing book by first sharing with you some background information about me.

I was born in a home where Jesus Christ, through the Holy Spirit, was already the master of the house. You know, one of those families where going to church was a norm, where all of you grew up to know just one pattern of life. The side of life I was exposed to growing up was those homes where we all wake up daily and gather together as a family, and say some prayers to God, and read few verses of Scripture. Well, most times, I attended the morning devotion half-awake with heavy eyes. I guess you can relate.

My parents are Presbyterian Christians. When I was growing up, people would come to our house very early in the morning to pray. At the time, I was four years old and would always sleep in the sitting room. When these people came to our house to pray, I would join them since my bed was in the parlor, and I would be unable to sleep again while they are praying to God.

I began to join them in the prayer session every day they came to the house, and I started feeling the presence of the Holy Spirit. I started to experience this divine feeling that I couldn't totally explain, but I couldn't ignore at the same time.

Gradually, it became a habit, which encouraged me to start reading the Bible even late in the night. I was very young and could not afford to buy a Bible for myself. However, since our house was a prayer house, my father had lots of Bibles, and I could easily make use of any of them each time I wanted to study. Before long, from the pages of scriptures,

I began to read different stories and got acquainted with the events around the lives of some Bible characters especially, Jesus Christ. This was how I came to connect with the Almighty, Jesus Christ.

My inquiry into the person and life of Jesus continued, but I knew deep within that something was missing. I knew I was yet to take a significant step, but I didn't really know how or what the step was, neither did I talk to anyone to assist me.

Fortunately, just like God heard my cry, suddenly, one faithful day, a group of people came to the little village where I was born to show a movie about the story of our Lord Jesus Christ, and I was opportune to watch the movie. In the movie, we saw Jesus Christ healing people and preaching the Gospel, then He got apprehended and was killed. On the third day, He rose from the dead and ascended into heaven.

After watching the movie, I became very emotional, and when I looked around, I could see how the movie had impacted most of the audience that day. Many of them burst into uncontrollable tears after seeking the gruesome sacrifice that Jesus paid for our sins. It was then; I came to the realization of my walk with God.

It was at this point that I decided to love and follow Christ with my whole heart. It was at that point that I understood the feeling I always have each time I read the Bible, and then the daily prayer now ministered more to me than just being a casual gathering of some Christian folks to fulfill an obligation to an unseen being. I drew closer to Jesus with more intent and purpose, and with the help of my late father, I grew stronger in faith.

At the time, one of the things I remember doing was helping my grandmother pay her tithes. She would send me to help pay her tithes whenever she had it. Also, the villagers gave a certain amount every month since the majority of the populace in our church, Presbyterian Church, were farmers.

I wanted you to know a little about my background before I dive deep into sharing my experiences and encounters with you.

Thank you for reading. God bless you.

Chapter Two

Sanctification When We Gather

Have you heard of "Presidential Advance Team"? It's a department in the president's security details whose responsibility is to visit a state or a country that the president will soon visit. They travel to the location weeks or months ahead to ascertain the safety and level of preparedness of the country for the arrival of Mr. President. Their recommendation is vital. If they give a negative report, the trip will either be canceled or a delegate will be sent on his behalf.

Now you may wonder how this even relates. The truth is God doesn't visit every man with his majestic presence just because some men and women gathered and are calling His name. Could it be that God also has some Advance Team that checks up on our gatherings before the Almighty visits? If they are, what would likely be the information they will look out for to approve such gathering to host the King of the Universe?

The Bible says that God is Holy and Holiness is a non-negotiable condition to host divine presence. The Bible says in 1 Thessalonians 4:3, "For this is the will of God, even your sanctification..." That is the desire of God is for us to be holy and sanctified at all times.

While growing up, I attended a lot of prayer groups, church services, conferences, and what stood out was that they all had similar methods to approach the Lord. Aside from the drums, songs, and other instruments. There was a unique pattern of worship in almost all the Christian gatherings I attended. And I believe that this method which the Lord taught me, will be very helpful to you, your prayer group, or church.

Now, the first thing we must do when we gather together in a meeting is to let the heavens and earth know why we've gathered. No doubt, God is all-knowing, but we must also signify our presence before God. This is a humble way of showing that we aren't gathered to see any man, we aren't gathered to chat and while away time, but we are gathered unto the Lord.

You see, many people assume that God knows we are in church, so He should manifest. Sorry to disappoint you, you may be wrong.

So, when you gather, this is how you should speak: "We have gathered here in the name of Jesus Christ to worship Him, to thank Him, and to praise His holy name because He is our God. Him alone we worship and praise in this house, room or place."

Then quote the Scripture that says, "For where two or three are gathered together in my name, there am I in the middle of them" (Matthew 18:20). The verse didn't say *when* but *where*. This goes to show that God is not bothered about the location but rather every place you gather to pray and worship God is convenient for Him to work wonders, only if you invite Him.

The Bible says in 1 Timothy 2:8, " I will therefore that men pray everywhere, lifting up holy hands, without wrath and doubting." So, we can lift our hands in worship everywhere, in your car, on the street, in the church building, in your house (like my father), but we must just invite Him if we want him to manifest His presence in our midst.

He said in the scriptures that when you invite Him, He will surely manifest by faith and practice to show that He's there. Now let's look at John 20:19-26:

Then the same day at evening, being the first day of the week, when the doors were shut where the disciples were assembled for fear of the Jews, came Jesus and stood in the midst, and saith unto them, Peace be unto you. And when he had so said, he shewed unto them his hands and his side. Then were the disciples glad, when they saw the LORD. Then said Jesus to them again, Peace be unto you: as my Father hath sent me, even so send I you. And when he had said this, he breathed on them, and saith unto them, Receive ye the Holy Ghost: Whose soever sins ye remit, they are remitted unto them; and whose soever sins ye retain, they are retained. But Thomas, one of the twelve, called Didymus, was not with them when Jesus came. The other disciples therefore said unto him, We have seen the LORD. But he said unto them, Except I shall see in his hands the print of the nails, and put my finger into the print of the nails, and thrust my hand into his side, I will not believe. And after eight days again his disciples were within, and Thomas with them: then came Jesus, the doors being shut, and stood in the midst, and said, Peace be unto you.

This means that He was already there in their gathering, and they could see Him. Here's another scripture that shows exactly what He does when He is in our midst.

An altar of earth thou shalt make unto me, and shalt sacrifice thereon thy burnt offerings, and thy peace offerings, thy sheep, and thine oxen: in all places where I record my name I will come unto thee, and I will bless thee.

Exodus 20:24

Making heaven and earth to your purpose keeps any other spirit illegal; it won't have any legal right to interfere in that prayer meeting.

Clean Up!

In addition to inviting Him into our gathering, the second thing to do is to make the place clean. There is a popular saying that cleanliness is next to godliness. A clean environment should be maintained if we want to see God manifest His presence. But God is Spirit; why does He care if the place is physically clean?

The Bible says in Exodus 19:10-11,

> And the LORD said unto Moses, Go unto the people, and sanctify them today and tomorrow, and let them wash their clothes, And be ready against the third day: for the third day the LORD will come down in the sight of all the people upon mount Sinai.

Here we see that God told them to maintain a clean environment to welcome His presence. He also commanded in Deuteronomy 23:12 that the toilet should be located far from the camp. These are not laws to keep up bound, but they are simply spiritual orders of worship, which help to prove that we are ready for the divine presence.

Moreover, as much as God desires a clean environment, more importantly, He wants a clean heart. And this is achieved by the blood of Jesus. I urge you all to start applying the blood in your soul, on your skin, and through every corner of your homes.

The blood of Jesus was shed to clean and sanctify us from our sins as God's children. It is a primary channel of sanctification. The Bible says Hebrews 9:22, "...without the shedding of the blood there is forgiveness of sin." But we must consciously plead the blood of Jesus to purge us and make us sanctified and to worship God. Nothing else but the blood of Jesus can purge us from inside out from dead and sinful acts so our worship can be acceptable in His sight.

Hebrews 9:14 says, "How much more shall the Blood of Christ, who through the eternal Spirit offered himself without spot to God, purge your conscience from dead works to serve the living God?" So, this is what you must say together; this house is sanctified with the blood of Jesus Christ. My body is sanctified with the blood of Christ.

Hebrew 10:10: "And by that will, we have been sanctified through the sacrifice of the body of Jesus Christ once for all." My mind is sanctified by the blood of Christ. We are justified by the blood. We are the holiness of God. "For thus says the high and exalted One Who lives forever, whose name is Holy, 'I dwell on a high and holy place, And also with the contrite and lowly of spirit In order to revive the spirit of the lowly And to revive the heart of the contrite'" (Isaiah 57:15).

We are the saints of God on earth. Also, during gatherings, we must confess our sins and apply the blood of Jesus. For the scripture all stated that "For all have come short His glory" (Romans 3:23).

Then, one person should stand and make this prayer:

"Holy Father, we have prepared your place, and we are inviting you to come and take your place in our midst. You are our Good Shepherd, and we ask that you be our pastor and take total control as we have gathered in this house.

"Oh Lord, come and receive our praise and worship. Talk to us, Lord, bless us and receive our offerings to you." When doing this, you can kneel or sit, but it will be good to kneel while receiving the King of kings. Then, tell the people that He is with them in the gathering and that with faith, they will be able to know that He is in their midst.

After this is done, then they can start to praise and worship His name with thanksgiving, believing that He will hear them.

Why Sanctification?

Hello, worshiper, I know you have a good voice, I know you a professional on the instrument, I know you are good with musical arrangements and sound mixing. So, you may wonder, why the fuse about sanctification? God inhabits the praises of the saints; why should we pay attention to being sanctified in His presence? Let me share a few truths with you.

1. **God is Holy**: The nature of God is holiness, and He will not lower His standard for anyone. And we must be holy as our Father is Holy. First John 3:3 says, "And every man that hath this hope in him purifieth himself, even as he is pure." Hope in this verse refers to the hope of believers to see God one day, to be in His presence. And John is saying, "If you want to see Him tomorrow, purify yourself today." The same goes for His presence in our gathering. His eyes are too holy to behold sinful men. But if we can only repent, He is willing to manifest in our midst.

2. **Only the Living Can Praise God**: Isaiah 38:19 says, "The living, the living, he shall praise thee, as I do this day..." The living refers to the man with the life of Christ. When a man embraces the finished work of Christ through His Blood, such a person becomes sanctified, then life begins. First John 5:12 says, "He that hath the Son hath life; and he that hath not the Son of God hath not life." God only responds to the worship of the living, not the dead.

3. **So he can hear our worship**: Of what use is a sacrifice that is not acceptable? Worship is referred to as a sacrifice. In Hebrews 13:15, the Bible says, "By him therefore let us offer the sacrifice of praise to God continually, that is, the fruit of our lips giving thanks to his name." This sacrifice is offered with our mouth. But it takes sanctification for God to hear whatever comes out of our mouth. How did I know? Scripture says in Isaiah 59:1-2, "Behold, the LORD's hand is not shortened, that it cannot save; neither his ear heavy; that it cannot hear: But your iniquities have separated between you and your God, and your sins have hid his face from you, that he will not hear." Sin blocks our worship from accessing God's ear and the sacrifice of our lips from being acceptable. But the good news is that we have the blood provision

to purify us so that we can align with the right order of acceptable worship.

So, wake up and seek sanctification above all things, even in your walk with God.

Chapter Three

What Is Praise?

I f you are used to Christian gatherings, you must have heard someone said at one point, "It's time to praise and worship God." Now, this is one common statement that spikes different responses in the heart of many. To some, it's time to listen to soft classical music; to some others, it's time to stretch out and sweat out because we are gonna dance, while to some, it's time to focus on God and how good He is.

Indeed the word *praise* is one of the Christian lingoes that many are over familiarizing with, and this has made it lose its potency in many of our gatherings. But, what does *praise* mean?

Christians often speak of "praising God," and the Bible commands all living creatures to praise the Lord (Psalm 150:6). One Hebrew word for "praise" is *yadah*, meaning "praise, give thanks, or confess." A second word often translated "praise" in the Old Testament as *zamar*, "sing praise." A third word translated "praise" as *halal* (the root of hallelujah), meaning "to praise, honor, or commend." All three terms contain the idea of giving thanks and honor to the one who is worthy of praise.

Furthermore, in the original Greek, *praise* means to tell of, to sing, to give, to be thankful for God's blessings, and to declare his goodness in our lives.

Praise is acknowledging the mighty acts of God in our lives.

The truth is, our lives are a catalog of God's goodness. Each day is a gift from God credited to us and just seeing the new day is enough to thank and praise God. An expression of that act is called *praise*.

From the Old Testament to the New Testament, men and women, at different levels, have demonstrated intense praises to God for His act in their midst as a group and their lives as individuals.

One of such was when the Lord delivered the children of Israel from the bondage of Egypt through the red sea after four hundred and thirty years of slavery. Many of them were born as slaves and died in slavery. It was as though the circle of servitude would never end. But one day, God came through and made over three million people walk on dry land through a sea that has an average depth of 490 m (1610 ft). The flip side of the event is that the same sea drowned their enemy.

When they got to the other side of the sea, the Bible says in Exodus chapter 15 that the people gathered and praised God for the great deliverance. They watched how the same sea parted for them until the elders and youngest among them passed through and swallowed and buried their enemies. "Then sang Moses and the children of Israel this song unto the LORD, and spake, saying, I will sing unto the LORD, for he hath triumphed gloriously: the horse and his rider hath he thrown into the sea" (Exodus 15:1).

They saw God's goodness, and their first response was praises to God. That deliverance remains the greatest in human history.

In another instance, we saw someone who called herself "a woman of sorrowful spirit." She was one of two wives of her husband, Elkanah, but she never had a child. The Bible recorded that she witnessed at least four christenings in the same house by her sister-wife, but she never had one. She was indeed a woman of sorrowful spirit.

She wept night and day and was mocked by her husband's wife, but one day God showed up for her. The Bible says in 1 Samuel 1:19, "and the Lord remembered her." She gave birth to a son to show that she acknowledged that it was God; she went openly and praised God.

Let's see 1 Samuel 2:1-5:

And Hannah prayed, and said, My heart rejoiceth in the LORD, mine horn is exalted in the LORD: my mouth is enlarged over mine enemies; because I rejoice in thy salvation. There is none holy as the LORD: for there is none beside thee: neither is there any rock like our God. Talk no more so exceeding proudly; let not arrogancy come out of your mouth: for the LORD is a God of knowledge, and by him actions are weighed. The bows of the mighty men are broken, and they that stumbled are girded with strength. They that were full have hired out themselves for bread; and they that were hungry ceased: so that the barren hath born seven; and she that hath many children is waxed feeble.

Psalm Of David

Moreover, the book of Psalms is an anthology of songs filled with praises to God. You may wonder why that is so; well, a brief background to the life of the writer may give us a hint.

David was the youngest son of Jesse and also a shepherd boy. As a teenager, he was exposed to dangers in the jungle that threatened his life. While his elder brothers were enlisted in the Israeli army, he was condemned to a time alone with the sheep in the bush.

Twice, he mentioned how he was attacked by wild animals that obviously came for his sheep but wouldn't have spared him either. But God saved him from the lion and the bear. He didn't just escape— God gave him the strength to overpower and kill a lion and a bear.

What more, while his brothers could boast of better prospects and opportunities to rise in the army and become more relevant and powerful in the society, what do you think is the future of a shepherd boy who reared the animals on behalf of the family?

However, from the backside, both in age and status, God brought him up. Suddenly, there was a vacancy in the palace, and a man that had no chance before became God's incontestable candidate. He was eventually anointed as king and moved from the bush to the palace.

Why won't such a man praise God?

Among the praises of the book of Psalms is Psalm 9:2, which says, "I will be glad and rejoice in you; I will sing the praises of your name, O Most High."

Psalm 18:3 says, "I will call upon the LORD, who is worthy to be praised: so shall I be saved from mine enemies."

Psalm 21:13 praises God both for who He is and for His great power. The Bible says, "Be exalted in your strength, LORD; we will sing and praise your might."

Psalm 136:1 (CEV): "Praise the LORD! He is good. God's love never fails."

Psalm 150 uses the term praise thirteen times in six verses. The first verse provides the "where" of praise—everywhere! "Praise God in his sanctuary; praise him in his mighty heavens." The next verse teaches "why" we must praise the Lord: "Praise him for his acts of power; praise him for his surpassing greatness."

Verses 3-6 note "how" to praise the Lord—with a variety of instruments, dance, and everything that has breath. Every means we have to make sound is to be used to praise the Lord!

Praise is indeed a means of expressing the goodness of God in the lives of His children. David didn't spare words, but He lavishly spoke of the goodness of God in His life, how God saved him from the sword of Saul, and many battles that came against him. He is indeed a classic example of a praiseful life in scriptures.

Like David and other men and women in the Old Testament, has God been good to you also? Has God elevated you from the back to the front? Have you experienced strange deliverance that you know can only be God? Then you have enough reasons to do something called "praise to God."

Hosanna in the Highest

Just like the Old Testament saints, in the New Testament, there are examples of praise that were given to Jesus (who is God the Son). Matthew 21:9 refers to those who praised Jesus as He rode a donkey into Jerusalem. The people have seen the great things he has done, and they all came out to sing His praise openly.

> And the multitudes that went before, and that followed, cried, saying, Hosanna to the Son of David: Blessed is he that cometh in the name of the Lord; Hosanna in the highest.

Also, in Matthew 8:2, Jesus healed ten lepers, and one of them returned and bowed before Jesus in worship.

In Matthew 28:17, the disciples of Jesus were said to worship Him after His resurrection. Jesus accepted praise as God.

The early church often shared in times of praise. For example, the first church in Jerusalem included a focus on worship (Acts 2:42-43). The church leaders at Antioch prayed, worshipped, and fasted during the time Paul and Barnabas were called into missionary work (Acts 13:1-5). Many of Paul's letters include extended sections of praise to the Lord (1 Timothy 3:14-16; Philippians 1:3-11).

At the end of time, all of God's people will join in eternal praise to God. "No longer will there be anything accursed, but the throne of God and of the Lamb will be in it, and his servants will worship him" (Revelation 22:3). With the curse of sin removed, those who are with the Lord will forever praise the King of kings in perfection. It has been said that our worship of God on earth is simply preparation for the celebration of praise that will take place in eternity with the Lord.

Experiencing His Manifest Presence

There is so much more to truly worshiping Jesus than church services and personal devotions. True worship requires a complete commitment of emotions, intellect, and will, and our reward is great. Carroll directs us into the presence of Christ by drawing on the Scripture, especially the book of Revelation, by giving practical steps of personal worship. The experiences of some of history's greatest saints also serve as relatable examples of what true worship entails.

What does it mean to worship God?

You are a chosen race, a royal priesthood, a holy nation, a people for his own possession, that you may proclaim the excellencies of him who called you out of darkness into his marvelous light.

1 Peter 2:9

Worship—to express honor to God through extravagant respect, reverence, and devotion.

What are you grateful for? When life is good, we tend to take basic things for granted, like having enough food and a safe place to sleep, enjoying good health and people who love us, etc. But research shows that being intentional to "count our blessings" makes our lives better.

Maybe you already practiced gratitude. Do you also reflect on where your good things come from? The apostle Paul reminded his friend, Timothy, that God "gives us all we need for our enjoyment" (1 Timothy 6:17, NLT). What can we do to respond to this truth?

Honor the Lord for the glory of His name. Worship the Lord in the splendor of His holiness (Psalm 29:2).

Think about this: God made His own universe. He built one of His planets with an atmosphere that could sustain life, where He placed humans and gave them everything they would ever need. And then, in spite of all our faults and failings (in fact, because of them), He invited us to join His family, adopting us as His daughters and sons. That's a very big reason to celebrate Him!

See what the Bible says in Psalm 8:1, 3-8:

Lord, you are our most powerful king. Your name is famous in all the whole world...When I look at your skies that your fingers made, I see the moon, I see the stars...Then I ask: Why do you remember men and women? What makes you visit them? You made their place a little below God...You made them to rule everything that your hands made. You put everything under their feet.

Chapter Four

Why Should We Praise God?

D r. Myles Munroe once said, "When the purpose of a thing is not known, abuse is inevitable." Now, that statement also applies to praise. A lot of Christians today see praise as an act of dancing and jumping to some melodious musical instruments without a clear understanding of what they are doing. Moreover, spiritual understanding is key to making the most of our walk with God.

Jesus gave a parable of the sower in Mathew chapter 13. My attention goes to the seeds that fell on good ground. I observed that even these grounds didn't bring forth the same harvest. Verse 23 stresses this point; it says, "But he that received seed into the good ground is he that heareth the word, and understandeth it; which also beareth fruit, and bringeth forth, some a hundredfold, some sixty, some thirty." Some brought forth thirtyfold, some sixty, and others a hundredfold returns. Why? Jesus said it is based on their level of understanding.

Purpose means the reason for which something is done or created. So purpose can also mean the spiritual understanding of an action. You see, like prayer, giving, salvation, and other scriptural truths, we need a clear and deeper understanding of what we should praise God if we must be profitable in our worship as a lifestyle.

A wise man once said, "Praise without meaning is empty." Hence, we must be sure our foundation while praising God is not based on our feeling or mood, but it must be grounded on the truth of God's Word.

I love what the Psalmist said in Psalm 47:6-7, "Sing praises to God, sing praises: sing praises unto our King, sing praises. For God is the King of all the earth: sing ye praises with understanding." He kept stressing that we should praise God, and you will think that's all he has to say until he added that in fact, it should be done with understanding, else it will be an effort in futility.

I believe that limited understanding of why we should praise is the reason most people don't even praise and worship God while others are not getting the required result. Now let me share with you some biblical reasons we should praise God to sponsor hope in you and a renewed commitment to a life of praise.

1. We Were Created to Worship.

Have you ever wondered what is going on in heaven, right? Now let's catch of glimpse of it from Revelations 4:8-11:

> And the four beasts had each of them six wings about him; and they were full of eyes within: and they rest not day and night, saying, Holy, holy, holy, Lord God Almighty, which was, and is, and is to come. And when those beasts give glory and honour and thanks to him that sat on the throne, who liveth for ever and ever, The four and twenty elders fall down before him that sat on the throne, and worship him that liveth for ever and ever, and cast their crowns before the throne, saying, Thou art worthy, O Lord, to receive glory and honour and power: for thou hast created all things, and for thy pleasure they are and were created.

Did you see that? Just as we understand that some angels are messengers to minister to the saints, and others are out to fight and defend the saints; likewise, there are angels in heaven whose responsibility is to keep praising God all through.

That is the reason God created you to replicate the happenings in heaven right here on earth. The Scripture says in Isaiah 43:21, "the people I formed for myself that they may proclaim my praise."

God's deepest intention while forming man was to put an entity on the earth who will praise Him in words and life like the angels do in heaven. So praise is your core responsibility on the earth.

2. It's a Commandment

Just like you know the commandment, "Thou shall not steal, thou shall not fornicate, thou shall not kill," it will interest you to know that "thou shall praise God is equally a commandment." Praising God is not a feeling but an instruction from God to all men. The Bible says in Psalm 150:6, "Let every thing that hath breath praise the LORD. Praise ye the LORD." In other words, so long we can breathe, we must acknowledge that blessing of breath by praising God and not complaining. The apostle Paul also wrote in one of his letters to the churches, "Rejoice in the Lord always: and again I say, Rejoice" (Philippians 4:4). And when Jesus was asked by His to teach them how to pray, He revealed the sandwich mature of our prayer. In Mathew 6:9-13, He commanded that we start with praise to God and equally end with praises to God. So when you don't praise God, you are disobeying one of His core instructions to man.

3. It is God's Habitat

Psalm 22:3 (WEB) says, "But you are holy, you who inhabit the praises of Israel." The greek word for inhabiting in that scripture means to dwell, to sit. In other words, just like water is the natural habitat for fish, the air or sky is the natural habitat for birds, and the land is man's natural habitat, God also dwells in praise. He seeks a place where He could live and always abide not to visit once in a while. Isn't that amazing? No wonder He pitches His throne in heaven because of the consistent praise and worship session up there. More so, you know that when God is with you, nothing can be against you.

4. It's a Debt We Owe God

Can man ever owe God anything? He owns all things and can access all things, so how can mortal man owe God? How does praise result in a debt we need to pay up? More so, to God! Now, let's glean from the story of the ten lepers from scriptures in Luke 17. One day, Jesus met ten lepers who pleaded to be healed, and then He instructed them to go and show themselves to the priest.
Miraculously, as they went, they were cleansed. Immediately one of them turned and ran back to Jesus, thanking and praising Him. Now let's see what Jesus said in Luke 17:17, "And Jesus answering said, Were there not ten cleansed? But where are the nine?" I can imagine Jesus standing by and watching them as they proceeded to the priest. But on the flip side, He was expecting them to come back in thanks and praise for what He has done for them. Friend, God has a record of His blessings in your life, He knows the number of good things He has done in your life, and He is waiting for you to pay off that debt. Clear your debt before God with thanksgiving and praise for all He has done for you, not some.

5. To Show Forth His Mighty Deeds and His Excellent Greatness

Psalm 150:2 says, "Praise him for his mighty acts: praise him according to his excellent greatness." A songwriter says, "Great is the Lord and greatly   to be praised." Imagine how you flaunt your beautiful car or your new gadget with numerous smart functions. We should also show forth the greatness of God on the earth by our praise.

6. His Unending Love and Mercy

Nothing gives value to life than salvation, and it is the peak of God's mercy towards man. No wonder the Bible says in Psalm 136:1,

"O give thanks unto the LORD; for he is good: for his mercy endureth for ever." His mercy is unending. He loves us with an everlasting love that is not anchored on what we did and didn't do. He just lloves us. The Bible stress this view in Lamentation 3:22-23, "It is of the LORD'S mercies that we are not consumed, because his compassions fail not. They are new every morning: great is thy faithfulness." So, when you think deeply about your past and how God still cleaned up your mess, then you should praise God.

7. To Stay Positive

Good news is hardly broadcasted on TV. We have been tuned to always enjoy listening to bad news and information all day so that you may begin to wonder if there is any good thing happening anywhere. We are all pushed by situations of life and circumstances that seek to cave us in despair. However, one of the ways to remain positive and sponsor hope in our every troubled heart is to praise God. You see, situations are subject to change, but God is the same yesterday, today, and forever. So it is wise to tag with a stable God rather than align with fluctuating circumstances. And one way to remain sane and insulated from the troubles of today is by praise.

8. It Shows We Trust God

One of the demonstrations of our faith and confidence in God is praise. It's easy to praise God when things are good and our plans are in alignment. But how easy is it to sing God's when the situation doesn't seem to be in your favor? Abraham was called a man of faith, and one of the ways he acted out his faith was a lifestyle of praise. The Bible records that over three servants were born in his house. By implication, he must have attended a minimum of three hundred christenings, sat there as the father of the house, and even some of the children will sometimes play around and call him grandpa, yet he had no child. Yet, he demonstrated his faith in God in regular praises to His Majesty. The Bible says in Romans 4:20, "He staggered not at the promise of God through unbelief; but was strong in faith, giving glory to God." Do you also believe God for that turnaround? That's enough reason to praise Him.

Chapter Five

Practical Ways We Can Worship God

Having found out why God expects us to worship, it's vital to also discuss the practical ways to praise and worship God. Let me start by saying that God will always seek to know our motive for everything we do. The Bible says in 1 Samuel 2:3, "for the LORD is a God of knowledge, and by him actions are weighed." So when we gather, or in our personal devotion, God is in our midst weighting our actions.

Many people and denominations have their personal thoughts and views about worship. But I'll like to share some biblical perspective that shows ways and postures of true worship.

1. Singing To God

This is perhaps the most common and undisputed mode of worship. Many times, we are intimidated by those that are gifted with melodious voices, and we think that until you have a voice like so and so, you can't praise God. Can I burst your burbles? God wants to hear you sing as you are. The Bible says in Ephesians 5:19, "Speaking to yourselves in psalms and hymns and spiritual songs, singing and making melody in your heart to the Lord;" No one is tagged in this instruction, every child of God can sing to God anywhere. David said, "I will bless the LORD at all times: his praise shall continually be in my mouth" (Psalm 34:1). That is, we can praise God anywhere, at all times. In your car, on the road, while you are walking out, in the restroom. Just open your heart to God and sing allowed from your heart. Your focus is God, not the people around you.

2. Raising Your Hands In Adoration

In Letters of Paul to Timothy, he said, "I will therefore that men pray everywhere, lifting up holy hands, without wrath and doubting" (1 Timothy 2:8). When a child wants you to pick him up, he will raise his hand to call your attention. Like a baby, lifting up holy hands is also a sign of surrender to God in true worship. David said in Psalm 141:2, "Let my prayer be set forth before thee as incense; and the lifting up of my hands as the evening sacrifice." It's a sign of intimacy and absolute surrender to the Lordship of God and His power.

3. Bow Down To Worship

Psalm 95:6 says, "O come, let us worship and bow down: let us kneel before the LORD our maker." Bowing down in worship is more than surrender but also a sign of reference to God. Most people think it's a show-off, but I say it takes a high level of humility to not care about your environment and still bow down in worship to God. When a man sees and recognizes how great God is compared to our humanity, yet He still wants to draw us closer, without any doubt, you will bow to worship.

4. Praising God By Dancing

Is it okay to dance in church? I think it's a sign of show-off. Well, these are some people's views. But the Bible says in Psalm 149:3, "Let them praise his name in the dance: let them sing praises unto him with the timbrel and harp." And in Psalm 150:4, "Praise him with the timbrel and dance: praise him with stringed instruments and organs." When David says we should praise God in a dance, you know it's not just an admonition, but an expression of his practice.

You remember when the children of Israel were bringing the Ark to its place, and David led the procession. The Bible says in 2 Samuel 6:14, "And David danced before the LORD with all his might; and David was girded with a linen ephod." He was not ashamed to dance with all his strength and sweat in worship before God. You see, perhaps you don't dance before God because you are bothered about those around you. David didn't care that the servants were there and the people; instead, he forgot his status and remembered where God took him from and danced vigorously. He told his wife that he played before God. Why are you conservative before your Father? Free up and let God accept your sacrifice of praise in a dance.

Conclusively, let me stress that God is seeking those that will worship Him in spirit and in truth. Singing or dancing is not to show that you can dance, but let your heart be fixed on God, let God be at the center of your worship and praise.

Chapter Six

Blessings in Praise and Worship

Praise is a kingdom mystery and also a spiritual weapon available for the saints. Rick Warren once said, "Happy moments, *Praise God*; difficult moments, *Seek God*; quiet moments, *Worship God*; painful moments, *Trust God*; every moment, *Thank God*." Rick recognized the blessings in praise, and he concluded that no moment is worthy of being secluded for praise; rather we should praise God always as the apostle Paul also admonished.

Praise and worship are a powerful part of our walk with God and are appropriate for our daily lives (1 Chronicles 23:30; Psalm 92:2; Psalm 59:16). It's commanded by God, but just like all the other things He tells us to do, it is followed by blessings. When we choose to worship in faith, despite our feelings, God sets in motion things only seen in the spiritual realm. What goes on in the spiritual realm will eventually show up for our eyes to see in the physical. All it takes is a believing heart that will glorify God in the best and the worst of times!

I read a story about the Duke of Wellington. He was the British military commander who led the army to defeat Napoleon at Waterloo. He was said to be an extremely difficult officer to serve with, brilliant yet demanding. One thing that was observed about him was that he rarely gave compliments to his soldiers even if they performed excellently and almost cut themselves into half. However, in his old age, when he was asked what he would have done differently if given a chance, he gave the following reply "I'd give more praise."

Why do you think the Duke gave such a reply? Perhaps he now understood the blessing and benefits of regular praises. That's why

I've reserved this chapter for exposing to you from scriptures some of the endless blessings that flow to you when you subscribe to praise, not as a Sunday service routine to commence the meeting but personally as a lifestyle.

Here are some benefits that follow through praise and worship. Put praise into practice and watch God's power work for you!

1. Invites God's Presence

We saw earlier from Psalm 22:3 that God dwells in our praise. In other words, when your life is void of divine presence or when you want God to show up in any situation, simply switch to praises.

In 2 Chronicles chapter 5, Solomon has completed the construction of the God's temple, and the Ark of the Covenant was already there. But something was missing— the presence of God! Without God's presence, the temple is just like any other building. But they knew better; they knew how to invite God's presence to overshadow and hallow the temple they have built. Let's see what they did in verses 11-14.

> And it came to pass when the priests came out of the Most Holy Place (for all the priests who were present had sanctified themselves, without keeping to their divisions), and the Levites who were the singers, all those of Asaph and Heman and Jeduthun, with their sons and their brethren, stood at the east end of the altar, clothed in white linen, having cymbals, stringed instruments and harps, and with them one hundred and twenty priests sounding with trumpets—indeed it came to pass, when the trumpeters and singers were as one, to make one sound to be heard in praising and thanking the Lord, and when they lifted up their voice with the trumpets and cymbals and instruments of music, and praised the Lord, saying: "For He is good, For His mercy endures forever," that

the house, the house of the Lord, was filled with a cloud, so that the priests could not continue ministering because of the cloud; for the glory of the Lord filled the house of God.

You want God to constantly dwell in your marriage, work and ministry? Then praise Him always.

2. Brings Victory

Life is a battlefield, and we must constantly maintain a battle-ready position. The devil is the arch-enemy of the saints, and he is consistently firing spiritual missiles just to steal, kill and destroy. But the good news is that we are redeemed as more than a conqueror, as victors and not victims, to command exploits and not to be exploited. And one of the ways to secure victory always and in every place against all the battles is to engage the armor of praise.

Let's read this passage in 2 Chronicles 20:15-24:

And he said, "Listen, all you of Judah and you inhabitants of Jerusalem, and you, King Jehoshaphat! Thus says the Lord to you: 'Do not be afraid nor dismayed because of this great multitude, for the battle is not yours, but God's. Tomorrow go down against them. They will surely come up by the Ascent of Ziz, and you will find them at the end of the brook before the Wilderness of Jeruel. You will not need to fight in this battle. Position yourselves, stand still and see the salvation of the Lord, who is with you, O Judah and Jerusalem!' Do not fear or be dismayed; tomorrow go out against them, for the Lord is with you." And Jehoshaphat bowed his head with his face to the ground, and all Judah and the inhabitants of Jerusalem bowed before the Lord, worshiping the Lord. Then the Levites of the children of the Kohathites and of the children of the Korahites stood up to praise the Lord God of Israel with voices loud and high. So they rose early in the morning and went out into the Wilderness of Tekoa; and as they went out, Jehoshaphat stood and said, "Hear me, O Judah and you inhabitants of Jerusalem: Believe in the Lord your God, and you shall be established; believe His prophets, and you shall prosper. And when he had consulted with the people, he appointed those who should sing to the Lord, and who should praise the beauty of holiness as they went out before the army and were saying: "Praise the Lord, For His mercy endures forever." Now when they began to sing and to praise, the Lord set ambushes against the people of Ammon, Moab, and Mount Seir, who had come against Judah; and they were defeated. For the people of Ammon and Moab stood up against the inhabitants of Mount Seir to utterly kill and destroy them. And when they had made an end of the inhabitants of Seir, they helped to destroy one another. So when Judah came to a place overlooking the wilderness, they looked toward the multitude; and there were their dead bodies, fallen on the earth. No one had escaped.

Did you get the picture? Three nations rose against Judah, and the King admitted that there was no way out for them, but then by divine wisdom, they set up singers to lead the battle, and God took over. Friend, you have tried; it's high time you handed over the battle to God. That issue is more than you, but not more than God. Amid the battles, take out time to sing praises and watch him fight for you, and you hold your peace.

3. Brings Deliverance From Enemies

David confessed in Psalm 3:1, "A Psalm of David, when he fled from Absalom his son. LORD, how are they increased that trouble me! Many are they that rise up against me. Many there be which say of my soul, There is no help for him in God."

Do you also have people against you in the place of your work? Are your families contending with you? Perhaps some people have looked at you and called you too weak to fight. I have good news for you: instead of crying and bowing in shame, sing aloud in adoration to the Monarch of the Universe. David was a man of war, but he showed us here that there were times that his enemies were too much for him to fight against. But he knew better. He said in Psalm 18:3, "I will call upon the Lord, who is worthy to be praised; So shall I be saved from my enemies." Just as he switched the gear to praise, his enemies were smitten before him. Why? His praise brings God down into his situation, and when God rises, all His enemies, including yours, will scatter.

4. Satisfies the Soul

Psalm 63:1-5:

O God, You *are* my God; Early will I seek You;

My soul thirsts for You; My flesh longs for You In a dry and thirsty land Where there is no water. So I have looked for You in the sanctuary, To see Your power and Your glory. Because Your lovingkindness *is* better than life, My lips shall praise You. Thus I will bless You while I live;

I will lift up my hands in Your name. My soul shall be satisfied as with marrow and fatness, And my mouth shall praise *You* with joyful lips.

5. Repels Depression

Too often, we allow unmet goals and failures of the past to affect our lives. Before long, we become depressed. And one of the signs of depression is a lack of joy and loneliness. But when you are given to praises, you can't be sad or depressed. Paul was arrested and imprisoned for preaching the Gospel; he was beaten, stoned, and left to die. Believe me, he was justified to be depressed. He should just sit at a corner and wonder why God allows him to go through such suffering. Yet in Philippians 4:4, he said, "Rejoice in the Lord always: and again I say, Rejoice." You can't praise God without a joyful heart. I'm saying to you also today, rejoice. That health challenge will soon turn around. Don't postpone your joy till you get that job or till you are confirmed pregnant. Take your eyes off the situation and see a good God ruling in your affairs.

6. Brings Liberty

Are you bound in shame, struck down with debt, or oppressed by the devil? Praising God is a key to total liberty. Paul and Silas were once arrested and kept in the inner prison. They were to be executed the next day, but that night they prayed to God for intervention. Nobody could set them free if God didn't show up. Just when they were done praying, they migrated into a session of intense worship and praised such that other prisoners heard them singing. Remember, God will always respond when praise goes up from a pure heart.

The Bible says in Acts 16:25-26.

> But at midnight Paul and Silas were praying and singing hymns to God, and the prisoners were listening to them. Suddenly there was a great earthquake, so that the foundations of the prison were shaken; and immediately all the doors were opened and everyone's chains were loosed.

Interestingly, as the majestic presence of God stepped into that prison, liberty was not just for Paul and Silas, but the experience impacted all other prisoners. Did I hear you say, "My situation is not physical; it's spiritual?" Even if it is psychological and you are bound in the chains of depression, if praise can break the physical chain, then yours is even easier. So, expect your liberty as you praise God.

7. Brings Joy

A session of praise is a moment when the aura of joy filled our hearts. A praiseful heart is a joyful heart. The Bible says in Psalm 100:4, "Enter into his gates with thanksgiving, and into his courts with Praise: be thankful unto him, and bless his name."

Psalm 16:11 also says, "Thou wilt shew me the path of life: in thy presence is fulness of joy; at thy right hand there are pleasures for evermore."

8. Draws Men To God

Praising God is lifting up the name of God from our hearts and our mouths. And Jesus said in John 12:32, "And I, if I am lifted up from the earth, will draw all peoples to Myself." Our heart is filled with divine presence when we praise, and we start to have a revelation of God more in our lives.

9. Strengthens Our Faith

Praise strengthens our confidence in God. You see, the Bible says without faith, it is impossible to please God (Hebrews 11:6). This goes to show that faith is the password to receiving anything from God. It is always a question of, "*Do you believe?*" Moreover, praise is one way to strengthen our faith in God. Abraham was a man of faith even in his trying times, yet he was a man of praise. No wonder how he could hold on in spite of challenges. Romans 4:20 says, "He did not waver at the promise of God through unbelief, but was strengthened in faith, giving glory to God."

10. It Leads To Multiplication

The major objective of any business of profit is the same in our lives. We want to have more money, more cars, build more houses, open more business units, have more children, and the bucket list goes on. But do you wonder what the contrary happens most times? It is because we complain about what we have rather than give God thanks for it. We despise what we have and fail to acknowledge the God that gave us, and by that ungrateful attitude, we shut the door from receiving more.

Let's see how praises and worship can multiply our blessing. Jesus finished a crusade with over 5000 people in attendance, and He felt the need to organize reception for the participants. But how will they get the food for such a crowd? Then a suggestion came that they had a boy with five loaves of bread and two fishes. What a suggestion! But instead of despising what was available, the Bible says that Jesus gave thanks, and it multiplied. Mathew 14:19 (GNT):

> He ordered the people to sit down on the grass; then he took the five loaves and the two fish, looked up to heaven and gave thanks to God. He broke the loaves and gave them to the disciples, and the disciples gave them to the people.

What was not sufficient became more than enough through the weapon of thanksgiving. So today, look that your account, look at your health, and thank God for it. And see how God ensures that what seems limited around you will continue to increase.

11. Leads To Restoration

What is dead and done around you? I have good news for you; it is coming back to life. Andrew Wommack once testified,

> I truly believe that my choice to praise God, even after getting the report that my son was dead, was one of the biggest factors in seeing him raised from the dead after nearly five hours. I didn't know what the outcome would be, but I started praising God with all of my heart and telling Him—and the devil—that regardless, I would not quit serving Him. It was at that moment that faith abounded in my heart, and I knew he would be raised from the dead.

Lazarus was dead and buried, but Jesus showed up four days after to raise him from the dead. Now, let's examine the lyrics of Jesus' prayer just when he was about to raise a man whose sisters had given up on him. John 11:41 says, "Then they took away the stone from the place where the dead was laid. And Jesus lifted up his eyes, and said, Father, I thank thee that thou hast heard me." Did you catch that? Perhaps Andrew Wommack only replayed what Jesus did, and like Lazarus, his son also came back to life. See, there is no hopeless case with praise. God will always show even in the most stinking and decaying situation. Just find the strength to praise Him.

12. Preserves Our Blessings

Like the gifts of God, His blessings in your life are also without repentance. It is not God's desire that you lose what He has given you. However, only God's hand can keep and preserve His blessing. And one way to ensure that His hand is upon your life and blessings to keep it is by thanking Him for Him always. See this warning in Malachi 2:2:

If ye will not hear, and if ye will not lay it to heart, to give glory unto my name, saith the LORD of hosts, I will even send a curse upon you, and I will curse your blessings: yea, I have cursed them already, because ye do not lay it to heart.

God cursed their blessings because they failed to acknowledge Him as the source of the blessing.

So quickly, praise God always for His blessings, that your car seems old, thank God you have a car, thank God for your health, and He will ensure that you are kept fit.

Chapter Seven
Acceptable and Declined Praise

Does God accept all worship? Does He dwell in the midst of all praises? The Bible says in Jeremiah 17:10, "I the LORD search the heart, I try the reins, even to give every man according to his ways, and according to the fruit of his doings." You see, the essence of worship is acceptance. If it is not acceptable, it will not be rewardable. Each time we spend in God's presence should be maximized because God does not call us to seek Him in vain.

When we gather in God's presence, there are commanded blessings available, so we must be positioned for proper alignment to enjoy the blessings of His presence. The Bible says in 2 Timothy 2:19, "Nevertheless the foundation of God standeth sure, having this seal..." God has a standard of worship; he has an order of acceptable worship which cannot be compromised for anyone. So, let's examine some points to not as we seek to render acceptable service to God.

1. Praise God in Holiness

Our praise is seen as a sacrifice, and it must be rendered in holiness if it must be acceptable. The Bible says in 1 Peter 3:12, "For the eyes of the Lord are over the righteous, and his ears are open unto their prayers: but the face of the Lord is against them that do evil." God's eye is upon only the righteous and ready to listen to them. Praises are seen as praying in song; if the prayer of the sinner is not acceptable, their praises cannot be acceptable. The truth is, you can't force your praise on God. The prayer of the sinner is an abomination to God; in the same vein, the praise and worship of a sinner is an abomination.

So, endeavor to clean up each time you appear before God. Don't assume you are positioned; ask for mercy so that your praises will not be a noise and your dance an exercise.

2. From the Heart

For your praise to be acceptable, it has to be from the heart. It should be heart-worship, not lip-worship. David said in Psalm 86:12, "I will praise thee, O Lord my God, with all my heart: and I will glorify thy name forevermore." Approach God's presence with your heart, not absent-minded. God seeks to know if you want to compete in dance, or you are indeed mindful of who He is and what He has done. The Psalmist also said in Psalm 103:1, "Bless the LORD, O my soul: and all that is within me, bless his holy name." Let everything inside of you praise the Lord in truth, not to please those around.

3. With Joy

Let me show you an interesting statement in Deuteronomy 28:47, "Because thou servest not the LORD thy God with joyfulness, and with gladness of heart, for the abundance of all things." Joy is key for your praise to be acceptable. I wonder how one can praise in sadness. People sing sad songs, but no one praises in sadness. So, maintain a heart of joy, maintain an atmosphere of joy, and rejoicing each time you are serving to praise God. Else it will not be acceptable.

Friend, in summary, acceptable worship is Christ-focused, not man. It is focused on the works and acts of God and nothing more.

Conclusion

Rolls-Royce Phantom VIII is a full-sized luxury saloon car with an inbuilt camera, four-wheel steering, silent-seal tires to reduce noise, a V12 engine and a speed capacity of up to 100 km/h. Imagine having such a machine in your garage, and you still choose to trek to your destination or struggle for a seat in public buses.

What a waste, isn't it? That's how knowledge is when you fail to utilize it.

You see, what you know doesn't change your situation but what you do with what you know. James said in James 1:25, "But whoso looketh into the perfect law of liberty, and continueth therein, he being not a forgetful hearer, but a doer of the work, this man shall be blessed in his deed." In other words, your transformation is in the application of the knowledge you gathered over time.

I believe you have been inspired by the insights in this book, so I want to admonish you to make the principles your way of life. Weigh your life with the lights from this book and make necessary amends in your worship from now. Nothing changes on its own; likewise, blessings don't jump at people—they flow when the conditions are met.

Make genuine worship your new lifestyle from now, not once and for all. Seek to serve and worship God always in spirit and in truth, and your life starts to reflect the blessings that accompany true worship.

God bless you!

CPSIA information can be obtained
at www.ICGtesting.com
Printed in the USA
LVHW022122070821
694771LV00012B/1255